Mark
ord
nter,
leeing

Emily
Berry
Stranger,
Baby

Du
Grü
Ash
Breakfast
Selected Poems
Translated by Michael Hofmann

G000043640

Poems

ff

ff

ff

ugust
einzahler
he Hotel
neira

Nick
Laird
Go
Giants

Lachlan
Mackinnon
The Jupiter
Collisions

Lachlan
Mackinnon
Doves

ff

Poetry

ff

Poetry

ff

dwin
Muir
elected
oems

Bernard
O'Donoghue
The Seasons
of Cullen
Church

W. H. Auden
Collected
Longer
Poems

Zaffar
Kunial
Us

Poetry

ff

Poetry

ff

ephen
pender
ew
ollected
oems

Wallace
Stevens
Selected
Poems

Jack
Underwood
Happiness

Adam
Zagajewski
Selected
Poems

ff

Poetry

ff

Poetry

ff

This diary belongs to

. . . .

First published in 2020
by Faber & Faber Ltd
Bloomsbury House
74–77 Great Russell Street
London WC1B 3DA

Designed and typeset by Faber & Faber Ltd
Printed in China by Imago

The colours of this year's diary are taken from the jacket design for
Tom Paulin's 1987 collection *Fivemiletown*

Clauses in the Banking and Financial Dealings Act allow the government
to alter dates at short notice

A CIP record for this book is available from the British Library

ISBN 978–0–571–35608–9

Faber
& Faber

Poetry
Diary
2021

Faber & Faber was founded in 1929 ...

... but its roots go back further to the Scientific Press, which started publishing in the early years of the century. The press's largest shareholders were Sir Maurice and Lady Gwyer, and their desire to expand into general publishing led them to Geoffrey Faber, a fellow of All Souls College, Oxford. Faber and Gwyer was founded in 1925. After four years Faber took the company forward alone, and the story goes that Walter de la Mare suggested adding a second, fictitious Faber to balance the company name.

In the meantime, the firm had prospered. T. S. Eliot, who had been suggested to Geoffrey Faber by a colleague at All Souls, had left Lloyds Bank in London to join him as a director, and in its first season the firm issued Eliot's *Poems 1909–1925*. In addition, the catalogues from the early years included books by Jean Cocteau, Herbert Read and Vita Sackville-West.

Poetry was always to be a significant element in the list and under Eliot's aegis Marianne Moore, Louis MacNeice and David Jones soon joined Ezra Pound, W. H. Auden, Stephen Spender, James Joyce, Siegfried Sassoon, D. H. Lawrence and Walter de la Mare.

Under Geoffrey Faber's chairmanship the board in 1929 included Eliot, Richard de la Mare, Charles Stewart and Frank Morley. This young team built up a comprehensive and profitable catalogue distinguished by modern design, much of which is still in print. Biographies, memoirs, fiction, poetry, political and religious essays, art and architecture monographs, children's books and a pioneering range of ecology titles contributed towards an eclectic list full of character. Faber also produced Eliot's groundbreaking literary review *The Criterion*.

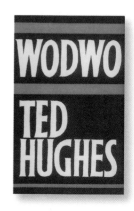

SYLVIA PLATH

winter trees

The Second World War brought both paper shortages and higher taxes, and the post-war years continued to be difficult. However, as the economy recovered a new generation of writers joined Faber, including William Golding, Robert Lowell, Ted Hughes, Sylvia Plath, Seamus Heaney, Philip Larkin, Thom Gunn and P. D. James. The publishing of Samuel Beckett and John Osborne began the firm's commitment to a modern drama list that now includes Tom Stoppard, Harold Pinter and David Hare.

From the 1970s through to the 1990s there was a blossoming in literary fiction, with the addition of authors such as Peter Carey, Kazuo Ishiguro, Barbara Kingsolver, Milan Kundera, Mario Vargas Llosa and Orhan Pamuk.

The year 2021 finds the publishing company that Geoffrey Faber founded remaining true to the principles he instigated and independent of corporate ownership. In over ninety years of publishing, Faber & Faber can count among its authors seven Carnegie Medal winners, three Kate Greenaway Medal winners, more than twenty Whitbread/Costa Book Award winners, seven Man Booker Prize winners, twelve Forward Poetry Prize winners, and thirteen Nobel Laureates.

Death of a Naturalist by Seamus Heaney

In addition to dedicated core publishing, recent years have seen some new strands emerge, including a distinctive Faber Audio list, the launch of the Faber Academy writing school and a Faber Members programme.

A more detailed chronology of Faber & Faber's poetry publishing appears at the back of this diary.

JANUARY

M	T	W	T	F	S	S
28	29	30	31	1	2	3
4	5	6	7	8	9	10
11	12	13	14	15	16	17
18	19	20	21	22	23	24
25	26	27	28	29	30	31
1	2	3	4	5	6	7

FEBRUARY

M	T	W	T	F	S	S
1	2	3	4	5	6	7
8	9	10	11	12	13	14
15	16	17	18	19	20	21
22	23	24	25	26	27	28
1	2	3	4	5	6	7
8	9	10	11	12	13	14

MARCH

M	T	W	T	F	S	S
1	2	3	4	5	6	7
8	9	10	11	12	13	14
15	16	17	18	19	20	21
22	23	24	25	26	27	28
29	30	31	1	2	3	4
5	6	7	8	9	10	11

APRIL

M	T	W	T	F	S	S
29	30	31	1	2	3	4
5	6	7	8	9	10	11
12	13	14	15	16	17	18
19	20	21	22	23	24	25
26	27	28	29	30	1	2
3	4	5	6	7	8	9

MAY

M	T	W	T	F	S	S
26	27	28	29	30	1	2
3	4	5	6	7	8	9
10	11	12	13	14	15	16
17	18	19	20	21	22	23
24	25	26	27	28	29	30
31	1	2	3	4	5	6

JUNE

M	T	W	T	F	S	S
31	1	2	3	4	5	6
7	8	9	10	11	12	13
14	15	16	17	18	19	20
21	22	23	24	25	26	27
28	29	30	1	2	3	4
5	6	7	8	9	10	11

JULY

M	T	W	T	F	S	S
28	29	30	1	2	3	4
5	6	7	8	9	10	11
12	13	14	15	16	17	18
19	20	21	22	23	24	25
26	27	28	29	30	31	1
2	3	4	5	6	7	8

AUGUST

M	T	W	T	F	S	S
26	27	28	29	30	31	1
2	3	4	5	6	7	8
9	10	11	12	13	14	15
16	17	18	19	20	21	22
23	24	25	26	27	28	29
30	31	1	2	3	4	5

SEPTEMBER

M	T	W	T	F	S	S
30	31	1	2	3	4	5
6	7	8	9	10	11	12
13	14	15	16	17	18	19
20	21	22	23	24	25	26
27	28	29	30	1	2	3
4	5	6	7	8	9	10

OCTOBER

M	T	W	T	F	S	S
27	28	29	30	1	2	3
4	5	6	7	8	9	10
11	12	13	14	15	16	17
18	19	20	21	22	23	24
25	26	27	28	29	30	31
1	2	3	4	5	6	7

NOVEMBER

M	T	W	T	F	S	S
1	2	3	4	5	6	7
8	9	10	11	12	13	14
15	16	17	18	19	20	21
22	23	24	25	26	27	28
29	30	1	2	3	4	5
6	7	8	9	10	11	12

DECEMBER

M	T	W	T	F	S	S
29	30	1	2	3	4	5
6	7	8	9	10	11	12
13	14	15	16	17	18	19
20	21	22	23	24	25	26
27	28	29	30	31	1	2
3	4	5	6	7	8	9

2020

JANUARY
M	T	W	T	F	S	S
30	31	1	2	3	4	5
6	7	8	9	10	11	12
13	14	15	16	17	18	19
20	21	22	23	24	25	26
27	28	29	30	31	1	2
3	4	5	6	7	8	9

FEBRUARY
M	T	W	T	F	S	S
27	28	29	30	31	1	2
3	4	5	6	7	8	9
10	11	12	13	14	15	16
17	18	19	20	21	22	23
24	25	26	27	28	29	1
2	3	4	5	6	7	8

MARCH
M	T	W	T	F	S	S
24	25	26	27	28	29	1
2	3	4	5	6	7	8
9	10	11	12	13	14	15
16	17	18	19	20	21	22
23	24	25	26	27	28	29
30	31	1	2	3	4	5

APRIL
M	T	W	T	F	S	S
30	31	1	2	3	4	5
6	7	8	9	10	11	12
13	14	15	16	17	18	19
20	21	22	23	24	25	26
27	28	29	30	1	2	3
4	5	6	7	8	9	10

MAY
M	T	W	T	F	S	S
27	28	29	30	1	2	3
4	5	6	7	8	9	10
11	12	13	14	15	16	17
18	19	20	21	22	23	24
25	26	27	28	29	30	31
1	2	3	4	5	6	7

JUNE
M	T	W	T	F	S	S
1	2	3	4	5	6	7
8	9	10	11	12	13	14
15	16	17	18	19	20	21
22	23	24	25	26	27	28
29	30	1	2	3	4	5
6	7	8	9	10	11	12

JULY
M	T	W	T	F	S	S
29	30	1	2	3	4	5
6	7	8	9	10	11	12
13	14	15	16	17	18	19
20	21	22	23	24	25	26
27	28	29	30	31	1	2
3	4	5	6	7	8	9

AUGUST
M	T	W	T	F	S	S
27	28	29	30	31	1	2
3	4	5	6	7	8	9
10	11	12	13	14	15	16
17	18	19	20	21	22	23
24	25	26	27	28	29	30
31	1	2	3	4	5	6

SEPTEMBER
M	T	W	T	F	S	S
31	1	2	3	4	5	6
7	8	9	10	11	12	13
14	15	16	17	18	19	20
21	22	23	24	25	26	27
28	29	30	1	2	3	4
5	6	7	8	9	10	11

OCTOBER
M	T	W	T	F	S	S
28	29	30	1	2	3	4
5	6	7	8	9	10	11
12	13	14	15	16	17	18
19	20	21	22	23	24	25
26	27	28	29	30	31	1
2	3	4	5	6	7	8

NOVEMBER
M	T	W	T	F	S	S
26	27	28	29	30	31	1
2	3	4	5	6	7	8
9	10	11	12	13	14	15
16	17	18	19	20	21	22
23	24	25	26	27	28	29
30	1	2	3	4	5	6

DECEMBER
M	T	W	T	F	S	S
30	1	2	3	4	5	6
7	8	9	10	11	12	13
14	15	16	17	18	19	20
21	22	23	24	25	26	27
28	29	30	31	1	2	3
4	5	6	7	8	9	10

2022

JANUARY
M	T	W	T	F	S	S
27	28	29	30	31	1	2
3	4	5	6	7	8	9
10	11	12	13	14	15	16
17	18	19	20	21	22	23
24	25	26	27	28	29	30
31	1	2	3	4	5	6

FEBRUARY
M	T	W	T	F	S	S
31	1	2	3	4	5	6
7	8	9	10	11	12	13
14	15	16	17	18	19	20
21	22	23	24	25	26	27
28	1	2	3	4	5	6
7	8	9	10	11	12	13

MARCH
M	T	W	T	F	S	S
28	1	2	3	4	5	6
7	8	9	10	11	12	13
14	15	16	17	18	19	20
21	22	23	24	25	26	27
28	29	30	31	1	2	3
4	5	6	7	8	9	10

APRIL
M	T	W	T	F	S	S
28	29	30	31	1	2	3
4	5	6	7	8	9	10
11	12	13	14	15	16	17
18	19	20	21	22	23	24
25	26	27	28	29	30	1
2	3	4	5	6	7	8

MAY
M	T	W	T	F	S	S
25	26	27	28	29	30	1
2	3	4	5	6	7	8
9	10	11	12	13	14	15
16	17	18	19	20	21	22
23	24	25	26	27	28	29
30	31	1	2	3	4	5

JUNE
M	T	W	T	F	S	S
30	31	1	2	3	4	5
6	7	8	9	10	11	12
13	14	15	16	17	18	19
20	21	22	23	24	25	26
27	28	29	30	1	2	3
4	5	6	7	8	9	10

JULY
M	T	W	T	F	S	S
27	28	29	30	1	2	3
4	5	6	7	8	9	10
11	12	13	14	15	16	17
18	19	20	21	22	23	24
25	26	27	28	29	30	31
1	2	3	4	5	6	7

AUGUST
M	T	W	T	F	S	S
1	2	3	4	5	6	7
8	9	10	11	12	13	14
15	16	17	18	19	20	21
22	23	24	25	26	27	28
29	30	31	1	2	3	4
5	6	7	8	9	10	11

SEPTEMBER
M	T	W	T	F	S	S
29	30	31	1	2	3	4
5	6	7	8	9	10	11
12	13	14	15	16	17	18
19	20	21	22	23	24	25
26	27	28	29	30	1	2
3	4	5	6	7	8	9

OCTOBER
M	T	W	T	F	S	S
26	27	28	29	30	1	2
3	4	5	6	7	8	9
10	11	12	13	14	15	16
17	18	19	20	21	22	23
24	25	26	27	28	29	30
31	1	2	3	4	5	6

NOVEMBER
M	T	W	T	F	S	S
31	1	2	3	4	5	6
7	8	9	10	11	12	13
14	15	16	17	18	19	20
21	22	23	24	25	26	27
28	29	30	1	2	3	4
5	6	7	8	9	10	11

DECEMBER
M	T	W	T	F	S	S
28	29	30	1	2	3	4
5	6	7	8	9	10	11
12	13	14	15	16	17	18
19	20	21	22	23	24	25
26	27	28	29	30	31	1
2	3	4	5	6	7	8

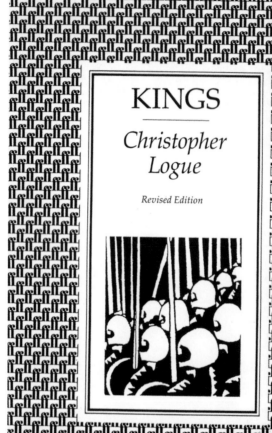

KINGS

Christopher
Logue

Revised Edition

28 Monday   BOXING DAY OBSERVED (UK, AUS, NZ)

---

29 Tuesday

---

30 Wednesday

---

31 Thursday   NEW YEAR'S EVE

---

1 Friday   NEW YEAR'S DAY (UK, IRL, AUS, ZA, NZ, CAN)

---

2 Saturday   3 Sunday

Annus Mirabilis

Sexual intercourse began
In nineteen sixty-three
(Which was rather late for me) –
Between the end of the *Chatterley* ban
And the Beatles' first LP.

Up till then there'd only been
A sort of bargaining,
A wrangle for a ring,
A shame that started at sixteen
And spread to everything.

Then all at once the quarrel sank:
Everyone felt the same,
And every life became
A brilliant breaking of the bank,
A quite unlosable game.

So life was never better than
In nineteen sixty-three
(Though just too late for me) –
Between the end of the *Chatterley* ban
And the Beatles' first LP.

The Complete Poems (2012)

4 Monday 2ND JANUARY HOLIDAY (SCT)
DAY AFTER NEW YEAR'S DAY (NZ)

5 Tuesday

Dentist   Di to Doctor

6 Wednesday

John to hospital

7 Thursday

8 Friday

Yoga?

9 Saturday   **10 Sunday**

Promenade

Openly wanting something
like the opened-up lungs of a singer.
I walk by the carriage of the sea
and the vinegar wind assaults.
Is this an age of promise? I blush
to want. If I were walking around
with you, arm in arm, along some
iron promenade, you could fill me up
with chocolate, you could push back
my cuticles with want. I'll just lie down,
my ribs opened up in the old town square
and let the pigs root through my chest.

Kingdomland (2018)

11 Monday

AP R. 00

12 Tuesday

12.25 Di to doctor

13 Wednesday

14 Thursday

15 Friday

yoga 12.00

16 Saturday　　　　　**17 Sunday**

Tinnitus: *January, thin rain becoming ice*

Now footsteps on shingle. Make of it what you will. Sea-birds roost
on the breakwaters, accustomed, of course, to twilight.
The spirit-lamp in that house on the headland could easily fall and spill
and the fire burn all night. Some time later, a subtle ghost,
yourself in memory perhaps, might well set foot
up there amid clinker and smoke, the whole place silent and still
except you bring in the *tic* of cooling timbers, and then the birds in flight.

*

Now chains through gravel. Make of it what you will.

Fire Songs (2014)

18 Monday

WAITROSE 9-10

19 Tuesday

Dot 10 . 00

20 Wednesday

Helen 10.00

21 Thursday

DOUG-DENTIST
MEDICINE DELIVERY

10.00 Helen

22 Friday

23 Saturday   **24 Sunday**

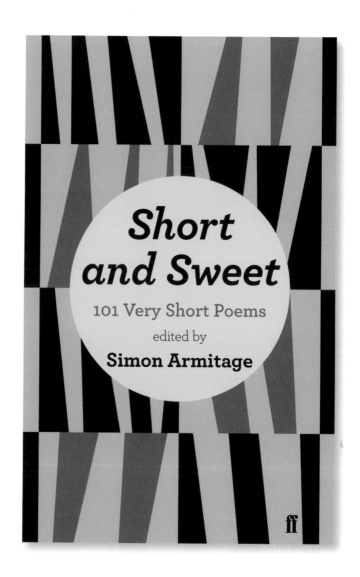

Short and Sweet

101 Very Short Poems

edited by

Simon Armitage

ff

25 Monday BURNS NIGHT

WAITROSE 9—10

6.00 Helen 2.3

Ocado

26 Tuesday AUSTRALIA DAY HOLIDAY (AUS)

27 Wednesday

28 Thursday

29 Friday

30 Saturday   31 Sunday

Sibelius and Marley

History is dismantled music; slant,
bleak on gravel. One amasses silence,
another chastises silence with nettles,
stinging ferns. I oscillate in their jaws.

The whole gut listens. The ear winces
white nights in his talons: sinking mire.
He wails and a comet impales the sky
with the duel wink of a wasp's burning.

Music dismantles history; the flambeaux
inflame in his eyes with a locust plague,
a rough gauze bolting up his mouth unfolds,
so he lashes the air with ropes and roots

that converge on a dreadful zero,
a Golden Age. Somewhere, an old film.
Dusk solders on a cold, barren coast. There
I am a cenotaph of horns and stones.

Ishion
Hutchinson
House of
Lords and
Commons

House of Lords and Commons (2017)

1 Monday

A.P. 11:30

2 Tuesday

3 Wednesday

4 Thursday

5 Friday

6 Saturday   WAITANGI DAY (NZ)   7 Sunday

The Rainbow

My heart leaps up when I behold
  A rainbow in the sky:
So was it when my life began,
So is it now I am a man,
So be it when I shall grow old,
  Or let me die!
The child is father of the man;
And I could wish my days to be
Bound each to each by natural piety.

Short and Sweet (2002)

8 Monday   WAITANGI DAY OBSERVED (NZ)

9 Tuesday

10 Wednesday

11 Thursday

12 Friday

13 Saturday   14 Sunday   VALENTINE'S DAY

Afternoon Tea

Please you, excuse me, good five-o'clock people,
I've lost my last hatful of words,
And my heart's in the wood up above the church steeple,
I'd rather have tea with the birds.

Gay Kate's stolen kisses, poor Barnaby's scars,
John's losses and Mary's gains,
Oh! what do they matter, my dears, to the stars
Or the glow-worms in the lanes!

I'd rather lie under the tall elm-trees,
With old rooks talking loud overhead,
To watch a red squirrel run over my knees,
Very still on my brackeny bed.

And wonder what feathers the wrens will be taking
For lining their nests next Spring;
Or why the tossed shadow of boughs in a great wind shaking
Is such a lovely thing.

POETRY PLEASE (2013)

15 Monday

16 Tuesday

17 Wednesday

18 Thursday

19 Friday

20 Saturday   21 Sunday

Andrew Motion

The Customs House

Poetry

ff

22 Monday

23 Tuesday

24 Wednesday

25 Thursday

26 Friday

27 Saturday   28 Sunday

The Knight's Tomb

Where is the grave of Sir Arthur O'Kellyn?
Where may the grave of that good man be? –
By the side of a spring, on the breast of Helvellyn,
Under the twigs of a young birch tree!
The oak that in summer was sweet to hear,
And rustled its leaves in the fall of the year,
And whistled and roared in the winter alone,
Is gone, – and the birch in its stead is grown. –
The Knight's bones are dust,
And his good sword rust; –
His soul is with the saints, I trust.

Short and Sweet (2002)

1 Monday ST DAVID'S DAY

2 Tuesday

3 Wednesday

4 Thursday

5 Friday

6 Saturday 7 Sunday

Before the War, We Made a Child

I kissed a woman
whose freckles
arouse the neighbors.

She had a mole on her shoulder
which she displayed
like a medal for bravery.

Her trembling lips
meant *come to bed*.
Her hair waterfalling in the middle

of the conversation meant
come to bed.
I walked in my barbershop of thoughts.

Yes, I thieved her off to bed on the chair
of my hairy arms—
but parted lips

meant *bite my parted lips*.
Lying under the cool
sheets. Sonya!

The things we did.

Deaf Republic (2019)

8   Monday

9   Tuesday

10   Wednesday

11   Thursday

12   Friday

13   Saturday   14   Sunday

Among the Narcissi

Spry, wry, and gray as these March sticks,
Percy bows, in his blue peajacket, among the narcissi.
He is recuperating from something on the lung.

The narcissi, too, are bowing to some big thing:
It rattles their stars on the green hill where Percy
Nurses the hardship of his stitches, and walks and walks.

There is a dignity to this; there is a formality –
The flowers vivid as bandages, and the man mending.
They bow and stand: they suffer such attacks!

And the octogenarian loves the little flocks.
He is quite blue; the terrible wind tries his breathing.
The narcissi look up like children, quickly and whitely.

Collected Poems (1960)

15 Monday

16 Tuesday

17 Wednesday   ST PATRICK'S DAY HOLIDAY (IRL, NI)

18 Thursday

19 Friday

20 Saturday   21 Sunday   HUMAN RIGHTS DAY

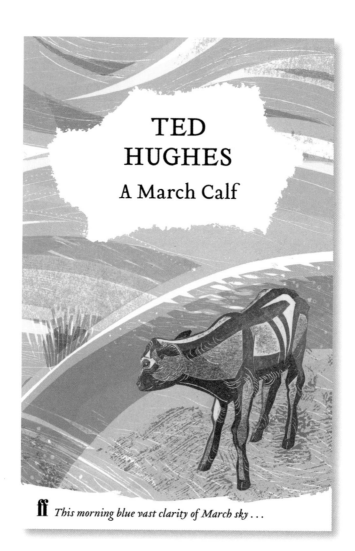

TED HUGHES

A March Calf

ff *This morning blue vast clarity of March sky . . .*

2 2 **Monday**   HUMAN RIGHTS DAY OBSERVED (ZA)

2 3 Tuesday

2 4 Wednesday

2 5 Thursday

2 6 Friday

2 7 Saturday   2 8 Sunday

from The Deserted Village

Sweet was the sound when oft at evening's close,
Up yonder hill the village murmur rose;
There as I past with careless steps and slow,
The mingling notes came softened from below;
The swain responsive as the milk-maid sung,
The sober herd that lowed to meet their young;
The noisy geese that gabbled o'er the pool,
The playful children just let loose from school;
The watch-dog's voice that bayed the whispering wind,
And the loud laugh that spoke the vacant mind,
These all in sweet confusion sought the shade,
And filled each pause the nightingale had made.
But now the sounds of population fail,
No chearful murmurs fluctuate in the gale,
No busy steps the grass-grown foot-way tread,
For all the bloomy flush of life is fled.
All but you widowed, solitary thing
That feebly bends beside the plashy spring;
She, wretched matron, forced, in age, for bread,
To strip the brook with mantling cresses spread,
To pick her wintry faggot from the thorn,
To seek her nightly shed, and weep till morn;
She only left of all the harmless train,
The sad historian of the pensive plain.

POETRY PLEASE (2013)

29 Monday

30 Tuesday

31 Wednesday

1 Thursday

2 Friday   GOOD FRIDAY (UK, AUS, ZA, NZ, CAN)

3 Saturday   EASTER (HOLY) SATURDAY   4 Sunday   EASTER SUNDAY

A Wagtail Sonnet

Full long thou bark'st at me, my love, and loud;
Hearing the sound, I do not miss the sense,
That I that once was lovingly bow-wow'd
Must now, unlov'd, bow out and hie me hence;
Loving the bark with which thou didst me woo,
I bark'd back lustily in loving wise,
Unwise though 't was to lend my love to you,
Who, now that love is loth, misprize the prize;
What is a bark but noise, a noisome sound,
Annoying and a nuisance to the ear,
Nagging the hearer, be he man or hound,
Who, hounded and unmann'd, cannot but hear?
    Words are more sweet, and here I proffer proofs,
    One witty word is worth a thousand woofs.

Old Toffer's Book of Consequential Dogs (2018)

5 Monday EASTER MONDAY (UK NOT SCT, IRL, AUS, NZ)
FAMILY DAY (ZA)

6 Tuesday

7 Wednesday

8 Thursday

9 Friday

10 Saturday   11 Sunday

To my Cottage

Thou lowly cot where first my breath I drew,
Past joys endear thee, childhood's past delight
Where each young summer's pictured on my view,
And, dearer still, the happy winter-night
When the storm pelted down with all his might
And roared and bellowed in the chimney-top
And pattered vehement 'gainst the window-light
And on the threshold fell the quick eaves-drop.
How blest I've listened on my corner stool,
Heard the storm rage, and hugged my happy spot,
While the fond parent wound her whirring spool
And spared a sigh for the poor wanderer's lot.
In thee, sweet hut, this happiness was proved,
And these endear and make thee doubly loved.

POET TO POET *John Clare: Poems Selected by Paul Farley* (2007)

12 Monday

13 Tuesday

14 Wednesday

15 Thursday

16 Friday

17 Saturday   18 Sunday

T. S. ELIOT / HELEN GARDNER

The Composition of

FOUR QUARTETS

Helen Gardner

19 Monday

20 Tuesday

21 Wednesday

22 Thursday

23 Friday   ST GEORGE'S DAY

24 Saturday   25 Sunday   ANZAC DAY

Höfn

The three-tongued glacier has begun to melt.
What will we do, they ask, when boulder-milt
Comes wallowing across the delta flats

And the miles-deep shag-ice makes its move?
I saw it, ridged and rock-set, from above,
Undead grey-gristed earth-pelt, aeon-scruff,

And feared its coldness that still seemed enough
To iceblock the plane window dimmed with breath,
Deepfreeze the seep of adamantine tilth

And every warm, mouthwatering word of mouth.

100 Poems (2018)

26 Monday   ANZAC DAY OBSERVED (AUS, NZ)

27 Tuesday   FREEDOM DAY (ZA)

28 Wednesday

29 Thursday

30 Friday

1 Saturday   WORKERS' DAY (ZA)   2 Sunday

Turning out

Turned the cows out two days ago.
Mailed with dung, a rattling armour,
They lunged into the light,
Kneeling with writhing necks they
Demolished a hill of soil, horning and
Scouring their skull-tops. They hurried
Their udders and their stateliness
Towards the new pasture. The calves lagged, lost,
Remembering only where they'd come from,
Where they'd been born and had mothers. Again
And again they galloped back to the empty pens,
Gazing and mooing and listening. Wearier, wearier –
Finally they'd be driven to their mothers,
Startling back at gates, nosing a nettle
As it might be a snake. Then
Finding their field of mothers and simple grass,
With eyes behind and sideways they ventured
Into the flings and headlong, breakthrough
Gallops toward freedom, high tails riding
The wonderful new rockinghorse, and circling
Back to the reassuring udders, the flung
Sniffs and rough lickings. The comforting
Indifference and contentment, which
They settled to be part of.

Ted
Hughes
Moortown
Diary

Moortown Diary (1979)

3 Monday   EARLY MAY BANK HOLIDAY (UK)
               MAY DAY (IRL)

4 Tuesday

5 Wednesday

6 Thursday

7 Friday

8 Saturday   9 Sunday

The bluebell horizontal

Deep woods.
Bright shallows overwhelming
a crowd of vertical tensions.

The Built Moment (2019)

10 Monday

11 Tuesday

12 Wednesday

13 Thursday

14 Friday

15 Saturday   16 Sunday

FOR THE TIME BEING

W. H. AUDEN

17 Monday

18 Tuesday

19 Wednesday

20 Thursday

21 Friday

22 Saturday   23 Sunday

Summer Shower

A drop fell on the apple tree,
Another on the roof;
A half a dozen kissed the eaves,
And made the gables laugh.

A few went out to help the brook,
That went to help the sea.
Myself conjectured, Were they pearls,
What necklaces could be!

The dust replaced in hoisted roads,
The birds jocoser sung;
The sunshine threw his hat away,

The orchards spangles hung.
The breezes brought dejected lutes,
And bathed them in the glee;
The East put out a single flag,
And signed the fête away.

POETRY PLEASE *The Seasons* (2015)

24 Monday

25 Tuesday

26 Wednesday

27 Thursday

28 Friday

29 Saturday   30 Sunday

Who killed these people?

Alex did,
with his left-the-gas-on breath.
    It was not me it was Annette
    who does not sleep.
    Through her door each night
    I hear the tearing human flesh.
Eczema is stress-related.
It flares up when I hear
our neighbour blitzing
his victims, calling it juice.
    That's your toxins talking.
    The culprit is Patricia who
    formaldehydes her fingernails
    so they look like pretty claws.
Please. The childless couple
at number ten make elderberry jam.
I've seen it hang in muslin
like a freshly popped-out eye.
    Come, let's point the finger
    at whichever finger pointed first.
    Now who of you was sensitive
    to my sweetheart's gas-leak breath?

Joe
Dunthorne
O
Positive

O Positive (2019)

31 Monday   SPRING BANK HOLIDAY (UK)

1 Tuesday

2 Wednesday

3 Thursday

4 Friday

5 Saturday   6 Sunday

'When to the Sessions of sweet silent thought'

When to the Sessions of sweet silent thought,
I summon up remembrance of things past,
I sigh the lack of many a thing I sought,
And with old woes new wail my dear time's waste:
Then can I drown an eye (unus'd to flow)
For precious friends hid in death's dateless night,
And weep a fresh love's long since cancelled woe,
And moan th'expense of many a vanished sight.
Then can I grieve at grievances foregone,
And heavily from woe to woe tell ore
The sad account of sore-bemoaned moan,
Which I new pay as if not pay'd before.
    But if the while I think on thee (dear friend)
    All losses are restor'd, and sorrows end.

POETRY PLEASE (2013)

7 Monday   JUNE BANK HOLIDAY (IRL)
             QUEEN'S BIRTHDAY HOLIDAY (NZ)

8 Tuesday

9 Wednesday

10 Thursday

11 Friday

12 Saturday   13 Sunday

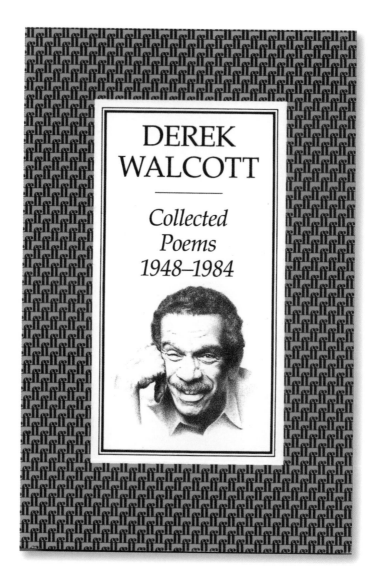

DEREK
WALCOTT

Collected
Poems
1948–1984

14 Monday

15 Tuesday

16 Wednesday   YOUTH DAY (ZA)

17 Thursday

18 Friday

19 Saturday   20 Sunday

High Summer

I never wholly feel that summer is high,
However green the trees, or loud the birds,
However movelessly eye-winking herds
Stand in field ponds, or under large trees lie,
Till I do climb all cultured pastures by,
That hedged by hedgerows studiously fretted trim,
Smile like a lady's face with lace laced prim,
And on some moor or hill that seeks the sky
Lonely and nakedly, – utterly lie down,
And feel the sunshine throbbing on body and limb,
My drowsy brain in pleasant drunkenness swim,
Each rising thought sink back and dreamily drown,
Smiles creep o'er my face, and smother my lips, and cloy,
Each muscle sink to itself, and separately enjoy.

POETRY PLEASE *The Seasons* (2015)

21 Monday

22 Tuesday

23 Wednesday

24 Thursday

25 Friday

26 Saturday   27 Sunday

The Air

What is this dark and silent caravan
that being nowhere, neither comes nor goes;
that being never, has no hour or span;
of which we can say only that it flows?
How was it that this empty datastream,
this cache of dead light could so lose its way
it wandered back to feed on its own dream?
How did that dream grow to the waking day?
What is the sound that fades up from the hiss,
like a glass some random downdraught had set ringing,
now full of its only note, its lonely call,
drawing on its song to keep it singing?
When will the air stop breathing? Will it all
come to nothing, if nothing came to this?

Don
Paterson
40 Sonnets

40 Sonnets (2015)

28 Monday

29 Tuesday

30 Wednesday

1 Thursday   CANADA DAY (CAN)

2 Friday

3 Saturday   4 Sunday

The Clod & the Pebble

Love seeketh not Itself to please,
Nor for itself hath any care;
But for another gives its ease,
And builds a Heaven in Hells despair.

So sang a little Clod of Clay,
Trodden with the cattles feet:
But a Pebble of the brook,
Warbled out these metres meet.

Love seeketh only Self to please,
To bind another to its delight;
Joys in anothers loss of ease,
And builds a Hell in Heavens despite.

5 Monday

6 Tuesday

7 Wednesday

8 Thursday

9 Friday

10 Saturday   11 Sunday

Kathleen Raine

Collected Poems

Poetry

ff

12 Monday BATTLE OF THE BOYNE HOLIDAY (NI)

13 Tuesday

14 Wednesday

15 Thursday

16 Friday

17 Saturday 18 Sunday

Que Sera

The song was 'Que Sera, Sera'.
We sang and sang it in the car
Till Daddy called a halt.

Fatalistic and carefree –
That wasn't him. It isn't me –
Worriers to a fault,

Always keen to organise
The future, though the enterprise
Is sculpting water.

It goes on flowing anyhow.
Daddy has no future now
And mine is shorter.

As my last years cascade away
Moving faster every day,
The song comes back to me,

Saying you can't change what's coming,
Just let go and keep on humming
What will be, will be.

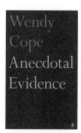

Anecdotal Evidence (2018)

19 Monday

20 Tuesday

21 Wednesday

22 Thursday

23 Friday

24 Saturday

25 Sunday

Up-Hill

Does the road wind up-hill all the way?
   Yes, to the very end.
Will the day's journey take the whole long day?
   From morn to night, my friend.

But is there for the night a resting-place?
   A roof for when the slow dark hours begin.
May not the darkness hide it from my face?
   You cannot miss that inn.

Shall I meet other wayfarers at night?
   Those who have gone before.
Then must I knock, or call when just in sight?
   They will not keep you standing at that door.

Shall I find comfort, travel-sore and weak?
   Of labour you shall find the sum.
Will there be beds for me and all who seek?
   Yea, beds for all who come.

POETRY PLEASE (2013)

26 Monday

27 Tuesday

28 Wednesday

29 Thursday

30 Friday

31 Saturday   1 Sunday

I

The chessmen are as rigid on their chessboard
as those life-sized terra-cotta warriors whose vows
to their emperor with bridle, shield and sword
were sworn by a chorus that has lost its voice;
no echo in that astonishing excavation.
Each soldier gave an oath, each gave his word
to die for his emperor, his clan, his nation,
to become a chess piece, breathlessly erect
in shade or crossing sunlight, without hours—
from clay to clay and odorlessly strict.
If vows were visible they might see ours
as changeless chessmen in the changing light
on the lawn outside where bannered breakers toss
and the palms gust with music that is time's
above the chessmen's silence. Motion brings loss.
A sable blackbird twitters in the limes.

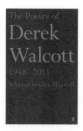

The Poetry of Derek Walcott 1948–2013 (2014)

2 **Monday** AUGUST BANK HOLIDAY (SCT, IRL)

3 Tuesday

4 Wednesday

5 Thursday

6 Friday

7 Saturday 8 Sunday

Julia
Copus
Girlhood

Poetry

ff

9 Monday NATIONAL WOMEN'S DAY (ZA)

10 Tuesday

11 Wednesday

12 Thursday

13 Friday

14 Saturday   15 Sunday

green

here's a plastic basket of polyester tulips
plus a heart-shaped card that sings I LOVE YOU
don't recycle them please
be happy with my pound-store presents

I stink I'm pretty sweaty I've been walking
this whole damp night to get here
let me curl around your converse cat-like
and dream of our cherry-days

maybe I could put my head still burning
from the memory of your hubba bubba kisses
onto your broad chest just till I feel a bit better
perhaps grab some shut-eye while you doze off

Soho (2018)

16 Monday

17 Tuesday

18 Wednesday

19 Thursday

20 Friday

21 Saturday   22 Sunday

The Way Through the Woods

They shut the road through the woods
Seventy years ago.
Weather and rain have undone it again,
And now you would never know
There was once a road through the woods
Before they planted the trees.
It is underneath the coppice and heath
And the thin anemones.
Only the keeper sees
That, where the ring-dove broods,
And the badgers roll at ease,
There was once a road through the woods.

Yet, if you enter the woods
Of a summer evening late,
When the night-air cools on the trout-ringed pools
Where the otter whistles his mate,
(They fear not men in the woods,
Because they see so few.)
You will hear the beat of a horse's feet,
And the swish of a skirt in the dew,
Steadily cantering through
The misty solitudes,
As though they perfectly knew
The old lost road through the woods . . .
But there is no road through the woods.

POETRY PLEASE *The Seasons* (2015)

2 3 Monday

2 4 Tuesday

2 5 Wednesday

2 6 Thursday

2 7 Friday

2 8 Saturday   2 9 Sunday

from Sonnets from the Portuguese

XLIII

How do I love thee? Let me count the ways.
I love thee to the depth and breadth and height
My soul can reach, when feeling out of sight
For the ends of Being and ideal Grace.
I love thee to the level of everyday's
Most quiet need, by sun and candlelight.
I love thee freely, as men strive for Right;
I love thee purely, as they turn from Praise.
I love thee with the passion put to use
In my old griefs, and with my childhood's faith.
I love thee with a love I seemed to lose
With my lost saints, – I love thee with the breath,
Smiles, tears, of all my life! – and, if God choose,
I shall but love thee better after death.

Winning Words: Inspiring Poems for Everyday Life (2012)

30 **Monday**   SUMMER BANK HOLIDAY (UK)

31 Tuesday

1 Wednesday

2 Thursday

3 Friday

4 Saturday   5 Sunday

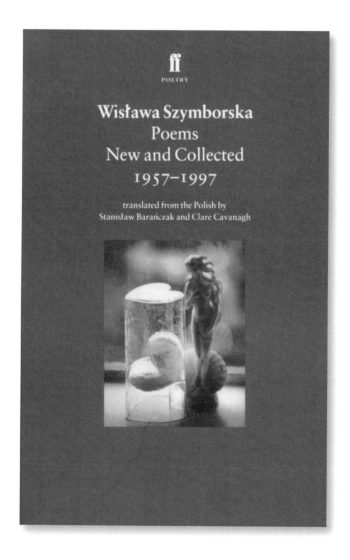

POETRY

Wisława Szymborska
Poems
New and Collected
1957–1997

translated from the Polish by
Stanisław Barańczak and Clare Cavanagh

6 Monday LABOUR DAY (CAN)

7 Tuesday

8 Wednesday

9 Thursday

10 Friday

11 Saturday   12 Sunday

The Great Horse of the World

The first thing I remember is being stepped on by a horse
while it paused to stale,
paying me no more heed
than it would an upset pail
of water or feed
or a comb dragged through the coarse
hair of its mane and tail.

The great horse of the world stamps and champs at the bit
and lays back one ear
as I approach
from the rear
to hitch it to the world-coach,
mindful of keeping at least one hand on it
so it knows I'm still here.

Frolic and Detour (2019)

13 Monday

14 Tuesday

15 Wednesday

16 Thursday

17 Friday

18 Saturday   19 Sunday

(Auto)biography

My detractors think they know me. Loud and always
too soft-hearted. The time I purchased fifty pairs of
frames from a sobbing woman whose eyewear shop
was closing down. The day I lost my father and cried
myself sick, until I thought I would never sing again,
though music was my only love during the revolution.
The time my daughter told me she was in love with a
woman and I lied and told her it would be OK. What
does three years of famine teach a person? Nothing.
Except that there is such a thing as perpetual hunger,
loss pounding on the windows like rain. Except that
my father loved me, and that he came back — as soon
as he could — in the swallowtail butterfly that fluttered
around the flat, in our pet Papillon, in my beloved child.

Flèche (2019)

20 Monday

21 Tuesday

22 Wednesday

23 Thursday

24 Friday   HERITAGE DAY (ZA)

25 Saturday   26 Sunday

Sonnet

Lift not the painted veil which those who live
Call Life: though unreal shapes be pictured there,
And it but mimic all we would believe
With colours idly spread,—behind, lurk Fear
And Hope, twin Destinies; who ever weave
Their shadows, o'er the chasm, sightless and drear.
I knew one who had lifted it—he sought,
For his lost heart was tender, things to love,
But found them not, alas! nor was there aught
The world contains, the which he could approve.
Through the unheeding many he did move,
A splendour among shadows, a bright blot
Upon this gloomy scene, a Spirit that strove
For truth, and like the Preacher found it not.

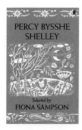

POET TO POET *Percy Bysshe Shelley: Poems Selected by Fiona Sampson* (2011)

27 Monday

28 Tuesday

29 Wednesday

30 Thursday

1 Friday

2 Saturday

3 Sunday

EZRA POUND

Collected Shorter POEMS

4 Monday

---

5 Tuesday

---

6 Wednesday

---

7 Thursday

---

8 Friday

---

9 Saturday   10 Sunday

Incantation

Because we time-travel into the future
at a blistering sixty minutes an hour,
I ask you to sit down and write me
one beautiful sentence I might carry
in my pocket on the journey when I go,
and in the window of the train unfold

O you were the best of all my days.

Never knowing if the thing is broken
or the door between us is still open,
you would like me to sit down and write
you one beautiful sentence you might
carry in your wallet when you leave,
and in the cab you take it out and read

Permit me voyage, love, into your hands.

Depending where one stands, each circle
back is a possible fall, a fail, a spiral,
and I would like you to take a few seconds
to write me out one beautiful sentence
to carry now across the night and ocean,
and held up at the gate I sit down and open

Everything was beautiful and nothing hurt.

Feel Free (2018)

11 **Monday**   THANKSGIVING DAY (CAN)

12 Tuesday

13 Wednesday

14 Thursday

15 Friday

16 Saturday   17 Sunday

Breake of Day

'Tis true, 'tis day; what though it be?
O wilt thou therefore rise from me?
Why should we rise, because 'tis light?
Did we lie downe, because 'twas night?
Love which in spight of darknesse brought us hether,
Should in despight of light keepe us together.

Light hath no tongue, but is all eye;
If it could speake as well as spie,
This were the worst, that it could say,
That being well, I faine would stay,
And that I lov'd my heart and honor so,
That I would not from him, that had them, goe.

Must businesse thee from hence remove?
Oh, that's the worst disease of love,
The poore, the foule, the false, love can
Admit, but not the busied man.
He which hath businesse, and makes love, doth doe
Such wrong, as when a maryed man doth wooe.

POET TO POET *John Donne: Poems Selected by Paul Muldoon* (2012)

18 Monday

19 Tuesday

20 Wednesday

21 Thursday

22 Friday

23 Saturday   24 Sunday

I Kicked a Mushroom

and then I felt bad.
And not just some cute toadstool or gnome's bed
but a fruiting body of brain-coloured disks
as wide as a manhole cover or bin lid,
a raft of silky caps basted in light rain
stemming from one root as thick as a wrist,
anchored in deep earth, like a rope on a beach.
One jab with a spade would have done the job,
then a pitchfork to hoik it over the hedge,
but I stuck in the boot then walked away
with its white meat caught in my tongue and lace.
All night it lies on the lawn inside out,
its tripes and corals turned to the stars,
gills in the air, showing the gods what I am.

The Unaccompanied (2017)

25 Monday OCTOBER BANK HOLIDAY (IRL)
LABOUR DAY (NZ)

26 Tuesday

27 Wednesday

28 Thursday

29 Friday

30 Saturday   31 Sunday HALLOWEEN

'Wild and wonderful . . . an
outrageous compound of critical cool
and rhetorical extravagance.'
Clive James,
TLS Books of the Year

READING

SHAKESPEARE'S

SONNETS

A New Commentary by

Don Paterson

'Soars above the competition . . . One of the finest living poets . . . brings
to this a craftsman's insight and refreshing candour.' *Independent*

ff

1   Monday

---

2   Tuesday

---

3   Wednesday

---

4   Thursday

---

5   Friday

---

6   Saturday   7   Sunday

On Being Asked for a War Poem

I think it better that in times like these
A poet's mouth be silent, for in truth
We have no gift to set a statesman right;
He has had enough of meddling who can please
A young girl in the indolence of her youth,
Or an old man upon a winter's night.

First World War Poems (2003)

8 Monday

9 Tuesday

10 Wednesday

11 Thursday   REMEMBRANCE DAY (CAN)

12 Friday

13 Saturday   14 Sunday   REMEMBRANCE SUNDAY

The Calling

the night is abrim with the in-between children
they are summoning Mother India

take us back   take us back   take us back

but the Motherland is piping the old grief
I was down on my knees   on my knees

why did you run for the towers
where the treasures of my heart are hanged

the night is abrim with the in-between children
their heads are down and they cry

take us back   take us back   take us back

our songs are afresh with the plough and the oxen
the smell of open fires where the naan is crackling

and our roses are the roses of home

British Museum (2017)

15 Monday

16 Tuesday

17 Wednesday

18 Thursday

19 Friday

20 Saturday   21 Sunday

Like the touch of rain

Like the touch of rain she was
On a man's flesh and hair and eyes
When the joy of walking thus
Has taken him by surprise:

With the love of the storm he burns,
He sings, he laughs, well I know how,
But forgets when he returns
As I shall not forget her 'Go now.'

Those two words shut a door
Between me and the blessed rain
That was never shut before
And will not open again.

Selected Poems (2011)

22 Monday

---

23 Tuesday

---

24 Wednesday

---

25 Thursday

---

26 Friday

---

27 Saturday   28 Sunday

TOM
PAULIN

*Selected Poems
1972-1990*

29 Monday

30 Tuesday   ST ANDREW'S DAY HOLIDAY (SCT)

1 Wednesday

2 Thursday

3 Friday

4 Saturday   5 Sunday

Birds at Winter Nightfall

Around the house the flakes fly faster,
And all the berries now are gone
From holly and cotoneaster
Around the house. The flakes fly! faster
Shutting indoors that crumb-outcaster
We used to see upon the lawn
Around the house. The flakes fly faster,
And all the berries now are gone!

6   Monday

7   Tuesday

8   Wednesday

9   Thursday

10   Friday

11   Saturday   12   Sunday

Aunt Helen

Miss Helen Slingsby was my maiden aunt,
And lived in a small house near a fashionable square
Cared for by servants to the number of four.
Now when she died there was silence in heaven
And silence at her end of the street.
The shutters were drawn and the undertaker wiped his feet—
He was aware that this sort of thing had occurred before.
The dogs were handsomely provided for,
But shortly afterwards the parrot died too.
The Dresden clock continued ticking on the mantelpiece,
And the footman sat upon the dining-table
Holding the second housemaid on his knees—
Who had always been so careful while her mistress lived.

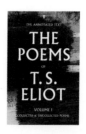

The Poems of T. S. Eliot Volume I (2015)

13 Monday

14 Tuesday

15 Wednesday

16 Thursday   DAY OF RECONCILIATION (ZA)

17 Friday

18 Saturday   19 Sunday

'The holly and the ivy'

The holly and the ivy,
When they are both full grown,
Of all the trees that are in the wood,
The holly bears the crown:

> *The rising of the sun*
> *And the running of the deer,*
> *The playing of the merry organ,*
> *Sweet singing in the choir.*

The holly bears a blossom,
As white as the lily flower,
And Mary bore sweet Jesus Christ,
To be our sweet Saviour:

The holly bears a berry,
As red as any blood,
And Mary bore sweet Jesus Christ
To do poor sinners good:

The holly bears a prickle,
As sharp as any thorn,
And Mary bore sweet Jesus Christ
On Christmas day in the morn:

20 Monday

21 Tuesday

22 Wednesday

23 Thursday

24 Friday   CHRISTMAS EVE

25 Saturday   CHRISTMAS DAY

26 Sunday   BOXING DAY /
DAY OF GOODWILL /
ST STEPHEN'S DAY

Poetry

Introduction·1

John Cotton,
John Daniel,
Douglas Dunn,
Elaine Feinstein,
Ian Hamilton,
David Harsent,
Jeremy Hooker,
V. C. Horwell,
Bartholomew
Quinn,

27 Monday   CHRISTMAS DAY OBSERVED (UK, IRL, AUS, NZ, CAN)

DAY OF GOODWILL OBSERVED (ZA)

28 Tuesday   BOXING DAY HOLIDAY (UK, AUS, NZ, CAN)

ST STEPHEN'S DAY OBSERVED (IRL)

29 Wednesday

30 Thursday

31 Friday   NEW YEAR'S EVE

1 Saturday   NEW YEAR'S DAY   2 Sunday

A Brief Chronology of Faber's Poetry Publishing

1925 Geoffrey Faber acquires an interest in The Scientific Press and renames the firm Faber and Gwyer. ¶ The poet/bank clerk T. S. Eliot is recruited. 'What will impress my directors favourably is the sense that in you we have found a man who combines literary gifts with business instincts.' – Geoffrey Faber to T. S. Eliot ¶ Eliot brought with him The Criterion, the quarterly periodical he had been editing since 1922. (The Waste Land had appeared in its first issue, brilliantly establishing its reputation.) He continued to edit it from the Faber offices until it closed in 1939. Though unprofitable, it was hugely influential, introducing early work by Auden, Empson and Spender, among others, and promoting many notable European writers, including Proust and Valéry. ¶ Publication of T. S. Eliot's Poems, 1909–1925, which included The Waste Land and a new sequence, The Hollow Men. ¶

1927 From 1927 to 1931 Faber publishes a series of illustrated pamphlets known as The Ariel Poems containing unpublished poems by an eminent poet (Thomas Hardy, W. B. Yeats, Harold Monro, Edith Sitwell and Edmund Blunden, to name but a few) along with an illustration, usually in colour, by a leading contemporary artist (including Eric Gill, Eric Ravilious, Paul Nash and Graham Sutherland). ¶

1928 Faber and Gwyer announce the Selected Poems of Ezra Pound, with an introduction and notes by Eliot. ¶

1929 Geoffrey Faber buys out Lady Gwyer and oversees the birth of the Faber and Faber imprint. Legend has it that Walter de la Mare, the father of Faber director Richard de la Mare, suggested the euphonious repetition: another Faber in the company name 'because you can't have too much of a good thing'. ¶

1930 W. H. Auden becomes a Faber poet with a collection entitled simply Poems. ¶ Eliot publishes Ash Wednesday. ¶

1933 Stephen Spender becomes a Faber poet with his first collection Poems, a companion piece to Auden's 1930 work of the same name. ¶ The first British edition of James Joyce's Pomes Penyeach is published. ¶

1935 The American poet Marianne Moore publishes with Faber. 'Miss Moore's poems form part of a small body of durable poetry written in our time.' – T. S. Eliot ¶ Louis MacNeice becomes a Faber poet. 'The most original Irish poet of his generation.' – Faber catalogue 1935 ¶

1936 The hugely influential Faber Book of Modern Verse (edited by Michael Roberts) is published. ¶

1937 *In Parenthesis* by David Jones is published. 'This is an epic of war. But it is like no other war-book because for the first time that experience has been reduced to "a shape in words." The impression still remains that this book is one of the most remarkable literary achievements of our time.' – *Times Literary Supplement* ¶ W. H. Auden is awarded the Queen's Gold Medal for Poetry. ¶

1939 T. S. Eliot's *Old Possum's Book of Practical Cats* is published with a book jacket illustrated by the author. Originally called *Pollicle Dogs and Jellicle Cats*, the poems were written for his five godchildren. The eldest of these was Geoffrey Faber's son Tom – himself much later a director of Faber and Faber. ¶

1944 Walter de la Mare's *Peacock Pie* is published with illustrations by Edward Ardizzone. ¶

1947 Philip Larkin's first novel, *A Girl in Winter*, is published. 'A young man with an exceptionally clear sense of what, as a writer, he means to do.' – *Times Literary Supplement* ¶

1948 T. S. Eliot wins the Nobel Prize in Literature. ¶

1949 Ezra Pound's *Pisan Cantos* is published. 'The most incomprehensible passages are often more stimulating than much comprehensibility which passes for poetry today.' – *Times Literary Supplement* ¶

1954 *The Ariel Poems* are revived with a new set of pamphlets by W. H. Auden, Stephen Spender, Louis MacNeice, T. S. Eliot, Walter de la Mare, Cecil Day Lewis and Roy Campbell. The artists include Edward Ardizzone, Edward Bawden, Michael Ayrton and John Piper. ¶

1957 Ted Hughes comes to Faber with *The Hawk in the Rain*. ¶ Siegfried Sassoon receives the Queen's Gold Medal for Poetry. ¶

1959 Robert Lowell's collection *Life Studies* is published. ¶

1960 Saint-John Perse wins the Nobel Prize in Literature. ¶

1961 Geoffrey Faber dies. ¶ Ted Hughes's first collection of children's poems, *Meet My Folks*, is published. ¶

1963 The Geoffrey Faber Memorial Prize is established as an annual prize awarded in alternating years to a single volume of poetry or fiction by a Commonwealth author under forty. ¶

1964 Philip Larkin's *The Whitsun Weddings* is published. ¶

1965 T. S. Eliot dies. ¶ Sylvia Plath's posthumous collection, *Ariel*, is published. 'Her extraordinary achievement, poised as she was between volatile emotional state and the edge of the precipice.' – Frieda Hughes ¶ Philip Larkin is awarded the Queen's Gold Medal for Poetry. ¶

1966 Seamus Heaney comes to Faber with *Death of a Naturalist*. ¶ Sylvia Plath's novel *The Bell Jar* is published by Faber. ¶

1968 Ted Hughes's *The Iron Man* is published. ¶

1971 Stephen Spender is awarded the Queen's Gold Medal for Poetry. ¶

1973 Paul Muldoon comes to Faber with his first collection, *New Weather*. ¶

1974 Ted Hughes receives the Queen's Gold Medal for Poetry. ¶

1977 Tom Paulin comes to Faber with his first collection, *A State of Justice*. ¶ Norman Nicholson receives the Queen's Gold Medal for Poetry. ¶

1980 Czesław Miłosz wins the Nobel Prize in Literature. ¶

1981 *Cats*, the Andrew Lloyd Webber musical based on *Old Possum's Book of Practical Cats*, opens in London. ¶

1984 *Rich*, a collection by Faber's own poetry editor, Craig Raine, is published. 'Puts us in touch with life as unexpectedly and joyfully as early Pasternak.' – John Bayley ¶ Ted Hughes becomes Poet Laureate. ¶

1985 Douglas Dunn's collection *Elegies* is the Whitbread Book of the Year. ¶

1986 Vikram Seth's *The Golden Gate* is published. ¶

1987 Seamus Heaney's *The Haw Lantern* wins the Whitbread Poetry Award. ¶

1988 Derek Walcott is awarded the Queen's Gold Medal for Poetry. ¶

1992 Derek Walcott wins the Nobel Prize in Literature. ¶ Thom Gunn's collection *The Man with the Night Sweats* wins the Forward Poetry Prize for Best Collection, while Simon Armitage's *Kid* wins Best First Collection. ¶

1993 Andrew Motion wins the Whitbread Biography Award for his book on Philip Larkin. ¶ Don Paterson's *Nil Nil* wins the Forward Poetry Prize for Best First Collection. ¶

1994 Paul Muldoon wins the T. S. Eliot Prize for *The Annals of Chile*. ¶ Alice Oswald wins an Eric Gregory Award. ¶

1995 Seamus Heaney wins the Nobel Prize in Literature. ¶

1996 Wisława Szymborska wins the Nobel Prize in Literature. ¶ Seamus Heaney's *The Spirit Level* wins the Whitbread Book of the Year Award. 'Touched by a sense of wonder.' – Blake Morrison ¶

1997 Don Paterson wins the T. S. Eliot Prize for *God's Gift to Women*. ¶ Lavinia Greenlaw wins the Forward Prize for Best Single Poem for 'A World Where News Travelled Slowly'. ¶ Ted Hughes's *Tales from Ovid* is the Whitbread Book of the Year. 'A breathtaking book.' – John Carey ¶

1998 Ted Hughes wins the Whitbread Book of the Year for the second time running with *Birthday Letters*, which also wins the T. S. Eliot Prize. 'Language like lava, its molten turmoils hardening into jagged shapes.' – John Carey ¶ Ted Hughes is awarded the Order of Merit. ¶ Christopher Logue receives the Wilfred Owen Poetry Award. ¶

1999 Seamus Heaney's *Beowulf* wins the Whitbread Book of the Year Award. '[Heaney is the] one living poet who can rightly claim to be Beowulf's heir.' – *New York Times* ¶ A memorial service for Ted Hughes is held at Westminster Abbey. In his speech Seamus Heaney calls Hughes 'a guardian spirit of the land and language'. ¶ Hugo Williams wins the T. S. Eliot Prize for his collection *Billy's Rain*. ¶ Andrew Motion is appointed Poet Laureate. ¶

2000 Seamus Heaney receives the Wilfred Owen Poetry Award. ¶

2002 Alice Oswald wins the T. S. Eliot Prize for Poetry for her collection *Dart*. ¶

2003 Paul Muldoon is awarded the Pulitzer Prize for Poetry for *Moy Sand and Gravel*. *Landing Light* by Don Paterson wins the Whitbread Poetry Award. ¶

2004 August Kleinzahler receives the International Griffin Poetry Prize for *The Strange Hours Travellers Keep*. ¶ Hugo Williams is awarded the Queen's Gold Medal for Poetry. ¶

2005 David Harsent wins the Forward Prize for Best Collection for *Legion*. ¶ Harold Pinter receives the Wilfred Owen Poetry Award. ¶ Charles Simic receives the International Griffin Poetry Prize for *Selected Poems 1963–2003*. ¶ Nick Laird wins an Eric Gregory Award. ¶

2006 Christopher Logue wins the Whitbread Poetry Award for *Cold Calls*. ¶ The Geoffrey Faber Memorial Prize is awarded to Alice Oswald for *Woods Etc.* ¶ Seamus Heaney wins the T. S. Eliot Prize for *District and Circle*. ¶

2007 Tony Harrison is awarded the Wilfred Owen Poetry Award. ¶ Daljit Nagra wins the Forward Prize for Best First Collection for *Look We Have Coming to Dover!* ¶ James Fenton receives the Queen's Gold Medal for Poetry. ¶

2008 Daljit Nagra wins the South Bank Show / Arts Council Decibel Award. ¶ Mick Imlah's collection *The Lost Leader* wins the Forward Prize for Best Collection. ¶

2009 Carol Ann Duffy becomes Poet Laureate. ¶ Don Paterson's *Rain* wins the Forward Poetry Prize for Best Collection, while *The Striped World* by Emma Jones wins the Best First Collection Prize. ¶

2010 *The Song of Lunch* by Christopher Reid is shortlisted for the Ted Hughes Award for New Work in Poetry and he is awarded the Costa Poetry Award for *A Scattering*. ¶ The John Florio Prize for Italian Translation 2010 is awarded to Jamie McKendrick for *The Embrace*. ¶ Derek Walcott wins both the Warwick Prize and the T. S. Eliot Prize for Poetry for his collection *White Egrets*. ¶ *Rain* by Don Paterson is shortlisted for the Saltire Scottish Book of the Year. ¶ Tony Harrison is awarded the Prix Européen de Littérature. ¶ The Keats–Shelley Prize is awarded to Simon Armitage for his poem 'The Present'. ¶ The Forward Prize for Best Collection is awarded to Seamus Heaney for *Human Chain*. ¶ Also shortlisted for the Forward Prize for Best Collection are Lachlan Mackinnon for *Small Hours* and Jo Shapcott for *Of Mutability*. ¶ The Centre for Literacy in Primary Education (CLPE) Poetry Prize is awarded to Carol Ann Duffy for *New and Collected Poems for Children*. ¶ Alice Oswald wins the Ted Hughes Award for New Work in Poetry for *Weeds and Wild Flowers*. ¶ *The Striped World* by Emma Jones is shortlisted for the Adelaide Festival Poetry Award. ¶ The Queen's Gold Medal for Poetry is awarded to Don Paterson. ¶

2011 *Of Mutability* by Jo Shapcott is the Costa Book of the Year. ¶ *Human Chain* by Seamus Heaney and *Maggot* by Paul Muldoon are both shortlisted for the *Irish Times* Poetry Now Award. ¶ *Night* by David Harsent is shortlisted for the Forward Prize for Best Collection. ¶ 'Bees' by Jo Shapcott is shortlisted for the Forward Prize for Best Single Poem. ¶ A new digital edition of T. S. Eliot's *The Waste Land* for iPad is launched, bringing to life one of the most revolutionary poems of the last hundred years, illuminated by a wealth of interactive features. ¶ The Queen's Gold Medal for Poetry is awarded to Jo Shapcott. ¶ At Westminster Abbey a memorial is dedicated to Ted Hughes in Poets' Corner. ¶

2012 *The Death of King Arthur* by Simon Armitage is shortlisted for the T. S. Eliot Prize. ¶ *The World's Two Smallest Humans* by Julia Copus is shortlisted for the T. S. Eliot Prize and the Costa Poetry Award. ¶ David Harsent's collection *Night* wins the International Griffin Poetry Prize. ¶ *81 Austerities* by Sam Riviere wins the Felix Dennis Prize for Best First Collection, one of the Forward Prizes for Poetry. ¶ *Farmers Cross* by Bernard O'Donoghue is shortlisted for the *Irish Times* Poetry Now Award. ¶

2013 The Forward Prize for Best First Collection is awarded to Emily Berry for *Dear Boy*. ¶ Hugo Williams is shortlisted for the Forward Prize for Best Single

Poem for 'From the Dialysis Ward'. ¶ Alice Oswald is awarded the Warwick Prize for Writing for her collection *Memorial*, which also wins the Poetry Society's Corneliu M. Popescu Prize for poetry in translation. ¶ The Queen's Gold Medal for Poetry is awarded to Douglas Dunn. ¶ The shortlist for the T. S. Eliot Prize includes Daljit Nagra for *The Ramayana: A Retelling* and Maurice Riordan for *The Water Stealer.* ¶ *Pink Mist* by Owen Sheers wins the Hay Festival Medal for Poetry. ¶ In his eulogy for Seamus Heaney, Paul Muldoon says, 'We remember the beauty of Seamus Heaney – as a bard, and in his being.' In November the first official tribute evenings to Heaney are held at Harvard, then in New York, followed by events at the Royal Festival Hall in London, the Waterfront Hall, Belfast, and the Sheldonian, Oxford. ¶

2014 Maurice Riordan is shortlisted for the Pigott Poetry Prize for *The Water Stealer.* ¶ Hugo Williams is shortlisted for the Forward Prize for Best Collection for *I Knew the Bride.* ¶ Daljit Nagra is awarded the Society of Authors Travelling Scholarship. ¶ Nick Laird's *Go Giants* is shortlisted for the *Irish Times* Poetry Now Award. ¶ Emily Berry, Emma Jones and Daljit Nagra are announced as three of the Poetry Book Society's Next Generation Poets 2014. ¶ *Pink Mist* by Owen Sheers is named the Wales Book of the Year after winning the poetry category. ¶

2015 *Fire Songs* by David Harsent is awarded the T. S. Eliot Prize for Poetry. ¶ Alice Oswald wins the Ted Hughes Award for New Work for *Tithonus*, a poem and performance commissioned by London's Southbank Centre. ¶ *One Thousand Things Worth Knowing* by Paul Muldoon wins the Pigott Poetry Prize. ¶ Don Paterson is awarded the Neustadt International Prize for Literature. ¶ *Terror* by Toby Martinez de las Rivas is shortlisted for the Seamus Heaney Centre for Poetry's Prize for First Full Collection. ¶ Paul Muldoon's *One Thousand Things Worth Knowing* is shortlisted for the Forward Prize for Best Collection. ¶ James Fenton is awarded the Pen Pinter Prize. ¶ *40 Sonnets* by Don Paterson wins the Costa Poetry Award, and is shortlisted for the T. S. Eliot Prize. ¶

2016 Don Paterson is shortlisted for the International Griffin Poetry Prize. ¶ *40 Sonnets* by Don Paterson is shortlisted for the Saltire Society Literary Awards. ¶ *The Seasons of Cullen Church* by Bernard O'Donoghue is shortlisted for the T. S. Eliot Prize. ¶ Jack Underwood receives a Somerset Maugham Award. ¶ An excerpt from *Salt* by David Harsent is shortlisted for the Forward Prize for Best Single Poem. ¶

2017 *The Unaccompanied* by Simon Armitage, *Stranger, Baby* by Emily Berry and *The Noise of a Fly* by Douglas Dunn all receive Recommendations from the Poetry Book Society. They also give a Special Commendation to *Selected Poems of Thom*

Gunn, edited by Clive Wilmer. ¶ Simon Armitage receives the PEN Award for Poetry in Translation for *Pearl* ¶ Bernard O'Donoghue's collection *The Seasons of Cullen Church* is shortlisted for the Pigott Poetry Prize. ¶ Emily Berry's collection *Stranger, Baby* is shortlisted for the Forward Prize for Best Collection. ¶ Sam Riviere's collection *Kim Kardashian's Marriage* is shortlisted for the Ledbury Poetry Prize. ¶ Douglas Dunn's collection *The Noise of a Fly* is shortlisted for the T. S. Eliot Prize. ¶ Paul Muldoon is awarded the Queen's Gold Medal for Poetry. ¶

2018 Matthew Francis's collection *The Mabinogi* is shortlisted for the Ted Hughes Award and Welsh Book of the Year. ¶ Toby Martinez de las Rivas's collection *Black Sun* is shortlisted for the Forward Prize for Best Collection. ¶ Richard Scott's collection *Soho* is shortlisted for the Forward Prize for Best First Collection, the T. S. Eliot Prize and the Costa Poetry Award. ¶ Owen Sheers is the recipient of the Wilfred Owen Poetry Award for 2018. ¶ Daljit Nagra receives a Society of Authors Cholmondeley Award. ¶ Seamus Heaney's collection *100 Poems* is shortlisted for the 2018 Books Are My Bag Readers Awards, Poetry category. ¶ Nick Laird's collection *Feel Free* is shortlisted for the T. S. Eliot Prize. ¶ Zaffar Kunial's collection *Us* is shortlisted for the Costa Poetry Award and the T. S. Eliot Prize. ¶ Hannah Sullivan's collection

Three Poems is shortlisted for the Roehampton Poetry Prize and the Costa Poetry Award, and goes on to win the T. S. Eliot Prize. ¶ Simon Armitage is awarded the Queen's Gold Medal for Poetry. ¶

2019 Simon Armitage is appointed Poet Laureate. ¶ Richard Scott's collection *Soho* is shortlisted for the Roehampton Poetry Prize and the Polari First Book Prize. ¶ Hannah Sullivan's collection *Three Poems* wins the John Pollard Foundation International Poetry Prize and is shortlisted for the Ted Hughes Award, the Seamus Heaney First Collection Prize and the Michael Murphy Memorial Prize. ¶ Sophie Collins's collection *Who Is Mary Sue?* is shortlisted for the 2018 Saltire Society's Scottish Poetry Book of the Year and wins both the Michael Murphy Memorial Prize and an Eric Gregory Award. ¶ Ishion Hutchinson's collection *House of Lords and Commons* wins the Windham-Campbell Prize. ¶ Lavinia Greenlaw's collection *The Built Moment* is shortlisted for the Roehampton Poetry Prize and the East Anglian Book Award (poetry category). ¶ Zaffar Kunial's collection *Us* is shortlisted for the 2019 Rathbones Folio Prize, the Roehampton Poetry Prize and the Michael Murphy Memorial Prize. ¶ 'The Window' from Mary Jean Chan's collection *Flèche* is shortlisted for the Forward Prize for Best Single Poem and her poem 'The Fencer' wins the Geoffrey Dearmer Prize. ¶ Poems from Rachael Allen,

Lavinia Greenlaw, Paul Muldoon and Hugo Williams are Highly Commended for the Forward Prizes for Poetry. ¶ Ilya Kaminsky's collection *Deaf Republic* is shortlisted for the Forward Prize for Best Collection, the T. S. Eliot Prize and the US National Book Award (poetry category). ¶

Acknowledgements

Poetry

All poetry reprinted by permission of Faber & Faber unless otherwise stated.

'Annus Mirabilis' taken from *The Complete Poems* © The Estate of Philip Larkin ¶ 'Promenade' taken from *Kingdomland* © Rachael Allen ¶ 'Tinnitus: January, thin rain becoming ice' taken from *Fire Songs* © David Harsent ¶ 'Sibelius and Marley' taken from *House of Lords and Commons* © Ishion Hutchinson ¶ 'Before the War, We Made a Child' taken from *Deaf Republic* © 2018 by Ilya Kaminsky. Reprinted with the permission of the Permissions Company, LLC, on behalf of Graywolf Press, Minneapolis, Minesota, graywolfpress.org. ¶ 'Among the Narcissi' taken from *Collected Poems* © The Estate of Sylvia Plath ¶ 'A Wagtail Sonnet' taken from *Old Toffer's Book of Consequential Dogs* © Christopher Reid ¶ 'Höfn' taken from *100 Poems* © The Estate of Seamus Heaney ¶ 'Turning Out' taken from *Collected Poems* © The Estate of Ted Hughes ¶ 'Bluebell Horizontal' taken from *The Built Moment* © Lavinia Greenlaw ¶ 'Who Killed These People' taken from *O Positive* © Joe Dunthorne ¶ 'The Air' taken from *40 Sonnets* © Don Paterson ¶ 'Que Sera' taken from *Anecdotal Evidence* © Wendy Cope ¶ 'I' taken from *The Poetry of Derek Walcott 1948–2013* © The Estate of Derek Walcott ¶ 'green' taken from *Soho* © Richard Scott ¶ 'The Great Horse of the World' taken from *Frolic and Detour* © Paul Muldoon ¶ '(Auto)biography' taken from *Flèche* © Mary Jean Chan ¶ 'Incantation' taken from *Feel Free* © Nick Laird ¶ 'I Kicked a Mushroom' taken from *The Unaccompanied* © Simon Armitage ¶ 'The Calling' taken from *British Museum* © Daljit Nagra ¶ 'Aunt Helen' taken from *The Poems of T. S. Eliot Volume I* © Set Copyrights

Picture credits

KINGS by Christopher Logue, design by Pentagram, illustration by Christopher Logue
Short and Sweet: 101 Very Short Poems edited by Simon Armitage, design by Faber
The Customs House by Andrew Motion, design by Faber, series design by Pentagram
A March Calf by Ted Hughes, design by Faber, illustration by Angela Harding
The Composition of Four Quartets by Helen Gardner, design by Berthold Wolpe

For the Time Being by W. H. Auden, design by Berthold Wolpe
Collected Poems by Derek Walcott, design by Pentagram, illustration by Sue Linney
Collected Poems by Kathleen Raine, design by Faber, series design by Pentagram
Girlhood by Julia Copus, design by Faber, series design by Pentagram
Wisława Szymborska Poems: New and Collected 1957–1997 translated from the Polish by Stanisław
    Barańczak and Clare Cavanagh, design by Pentagram
Collected Shorter Poems by Ezra Pound, design by Berthold Wolpe
Reading Shakespeare's Sonnets by Don Paterson, design by Faber, illustration by Eleanor Crow
Selected Poems 1972–1990 by Tom Paulin, design by Pentagram, illustration by Sue Linney
Poetry Introduction 1, design by Shirley Tucker

NOTES

NOTES

FABER ACADEMY

Kickstart your writing life with a course at Faber & Faber, the home of British poetry

From our one-day Start to Write Poetry course to our twelve-week Poetry Salon, we have something for poets at all stages of their writing journey. And for those not looking for a course, we also offer a range of manuscript assessments – get professional feedback on your work from a published poet, with a deep knowledge of the industry and a passion for the craft of writing poetry.

TO FIND OUT MORE
VISIT FABERACADEMY.CO.UK

MEMBERS

FABER

Become a Faber Member and discover the best in the arts and literature.

Sign up to the Faber Members programme and enjoy specially curated events, tailored discounts, and exclusive previews of our forthcoming publications from the best novelists, poets, playwrights, thinkers, musicians and artists.

ff

Join for free today at faber.co.uk/members

Eiléan Ní Chuilleanáin Selected Poems

Amy Clampitt Collected Poems

Douglas Dunn New Selected Poems 1964–1999

Lawrenc Durrell Selected Poems

Edited by Peter Porter

Julia Copus Girlhood

Michael Hofmann Selected Poems

Mick Imlah Selected Poems

Keith Douglas Complet Poems

Sam Riviere Kim Kardashian's Marriage

Jamie McKendrick Anomaly

Sophie Collins Who Is Mary Sue?

Doroth Molloy Hare Soup

Tom Paulin New Selected Poems

Maurice Riordan The Holy Land

Frederick Seidel Peaches Goes It Alone

Charles Simic Selected Poems 1963–2003